Discovered
Passion

Rhontina Burroughs

Order this book online at www.trafford.com
or email orders@trafford.com

Most Trafford titles are also available at major online book retailers.

Scripture quotations marked NIV are taken from the *Holy Bible, New
International Version*®. *NIV*®. Copyright © 1973, 1978, 1984 by International
Bible Society. Used by permission of Zondervan. All rights reserved. [Biblica]

Print information available on the last page.

ISBN: 978-1-4907-7308-7 (sc)
ISBN: 978-1-4907-7307-0 (hc)
ISBN: 978-1-4907-7309-4 (e)

Library of Congress Control Number: 2016907083

Trafford rev. 05/04/2016

www.trafford.com
North America & international
toll-free: 1 888 232 4444 (USA & Canada)
fax: 812 355 4082

CONTENTS

JOURNEY 1

AT ODDS 3
Before I Formed You, I Knew You ~Psalm 139:1 4
Searching 5
The Redemption 6
The Locksmith 7
Dear Love 8
Again 9

JOURNEY 2

AT ODDS PT 2 12
Spiritual Math 13
Discovered Passion 15
Multiple 16
Stepping Out 17
Thinking 18
Original Origin 19

JOURNEY 3

Fear 23
Pregnant with a cause 25
THE CHOICE 26
Season, Seasoning, Seasoned 28
The Garden 30
A Divine Appointment 32
AM I MY SISTAHS KEEPER? 33
Encouraging One Another 35
The Great Command 36
We are History 37
There's Victory in Me 39

Friends 40
HEAVEN 42
Dedicated to Mack Hankerson 43
Longevity.. 44
Rooted and Grounded in Love...45
Living the Golden Life... 46
The Calling 47
Prepared..49
VICTORY 50

JOURNEY 4

Desired 53
Coffee 54
The Dilemma..56
Don't Wanna Beg...57
Angel 58
Clueless...59
Invitation 60
Anatomy 61
Child's Play...62
For you.. 64
FRESH EYES..65
I Wonder.. 66
Afraid..67
I Am your Man...68
I Am Your Woman..69
iNsAtIaBlE mE...70
Lifetime 71
Yesterday, Today, Tomorrow...72
Loving You..73
Me and You...74
Meeting 75
Merger 76
Mirror, Mirror 77
My Life to You..78
No more..79
Realization 80

Shame you lost me 81
The Difference...82
The Man, His Lady, Their Country.............................84
Together...85
Unfinished 86
Who AM I?..87
Wondering...88
Yearning..89
Your Girl.. 90
Sayonara..91

Dedicated to:

My father, Harry Burroughs
My Uncle, Edward Hughes
And Best Friend, Fanette Tate

ACKNOWLEDGEMENTS

I would like to thank my Heavenly Father, for depositing the gifts and talents within me to share. For showing me that if I trust Him and believe in Him, He will give me the desires of my heart. I am truly humbled by your goodness.

Thank you, to my parents for all that they have done, given and sacrificed for me. Without your love and support, this chapter of my life would not be reached.

Thank You, to all of my family and friends who have prayed with me, encouraged me, and motivated me to step out of the shadows and into the light of my purpose.

I Love you all!

Rhontina

EACH CHAPTER BEGINS A JOURNEY

Journey 1:

Begins with being at odds with emotional turmoil and reveals God's unconditional love. Sometimes God has to take you through some things to get your attention.

Journey 2

Once you come to the realization that God truly loves and wants the best for you, the plans He has for your life will begin to unfold.

Journey 3

Inspiration: Shares insightful essays on various topics.

Journey 4:

Expresses the desire for love the way it was designed to be. Love is beautiful, passionate, intimate, open and honest with the person God fashioned just for you.

JOURNEY 1

AT ODDS

INTRODUCTION

Somewhere in my search for love and fulfillment I lost me! Last time I checked, me was infused inside. Me went everywhere I went, me was always there. Me enjoyed painting, writing, and reading, in general, exploring her creative side. I enjoyed that about her. She was always finding things to create mold or sculpt. She would become mesmerized by the awesomeness of things and how they worked. She was always reading and developing her intuitive side. Oh me, (the other me) was more content with finding love instead of letting love search for me. I told me that we needed to separate, to explore different avenues. Me resisted, I became selfish and forced me to give up the things that made her special and unique. I made her feel guilty about being creative, telling her that no man wanted a creative woman spending all of her time drawing, painting, writing poems and such. "That's childish! Who wants your stuff about love anyway I said". That devastated me. I and me separated. I don't know where me went. I LOST ME in the midst of hurtful relationships, excess weight gain and merely hiding. I miss me! I miss that side of me that became overjoyed when I painted a piece of ceramic or wrote a poem. I miss that creative talented side that God so graciously blessed me with. When I find me again, you can best believe that will be a joyous occasion. I pray my God will help me to find and reunite me to the other me, because I am absolutely lost without her!

R. Burroughs

BEFORE I FORMED YOU, I KNEW YOU ~PSALM 139:1

My Child,

Do you know who I am? I am God! I am your God! I formed you. I gave you life. I gave you your color, your height, your weight; I even know how many hairs you have on your head. I designed you exactly the way I wanted you to be. You are special and unique. You are love, formed from my love. You are beautiful. It hurts me when you look in the mirror at yourself and say that you are not beautiful! It hurts me when you hold high esteem for others and not yourself. Do you know what you are saying about me? It hurts me when you accept what others say about you and not what I AM says about you. It hurts me when I see you cry because others cannot, will not, or accept you for who I made you to be. You are an original. There is no one like you. I FORMED you. I put you on this earth because I wanted you here. You have a purpose and a destiny. I gave it to you. No one understands you like I do, no one knows your moods, pains, joys and excitements the way I do. I made you. Why do you seek others to learn about you? Why do you seek outside sources when I am the only source you need? I love you! I am repeating this to you, because I want you to see just how much you mean to me. I took the time to create you; I took the time to breathe into you. You are my child, your are my princess, heir to my throne. Pick yourself up and receive my grace. I am your God!

Rhontina Burroughs

SEARCHING

My child, I have been looking for you. Where have you been? I miss you. You have been running afraid to face your fears. How many times do I need to show you that I will never leave you? I know that there are times when you feel as if I am nor there, but I am. Every time you breathe, you are breathing in my essence, my force, the force that created you and gave you a destiny to accomplish. Every time you call out my name, your voice is amplified, it reaches to the far depths of my soul and I come to your side; lifting you, and encouraging you.

My child, I love you. Please trust me. I am greater than your biggest fears. Remember I died for you so that you may live free.

My child, seek me, pray to me, praise me with all that you do, love me with all of your heart. Do not be afraid. I am always with you

THE REDEMPTION

I was sinking deep in my turmoil and sins. I was joyless because of the wrong choices I put my mind and spirit in. I was saved but somewhere in my life I lost my focus, I didn't know the purpose that God created deep within. Not knowing where to go or where to turn, I internalized my hurt and caused my heart to burn. My life was caving in, my soul was bruised and lost, no other option did I have but to go to the cross. With my burdens in tow; my back weary from the heavy load. I gently laid my baggage's down. Bag number one; my childhood hurts. Bag number two, my teenage pains, bag number three, my adult failures and ruined relationships. With tears streaming down my face, the clouds of doubt began to set in. I wondered if I came to the right place. I cried "Oh Lord, please release this pain I feel, renew my life and spirit; give it zeal". I knelt down, my face buried in the ground. The blood that Christ shed –gently fell and caressed the top of my head. I looked up again at the man whose arms were stretched wide; I glanced at the wound from where the sword pierced his side. He opened his eyes and said to me, "my child, I am here dying for you to set you free. Do not wonder anymore if you are at the right place. Look into my eyes and see that all you've been through is now and will forever be replaced. My love for you is great you see, No one in the world can love you, shed my life for you and redeem you like me. Leave the burdens of your heart and mind with me. My blood is redemptive. It cleanses you from the top of your head to the souls of your feet. It uplifts your spirit and gives you comforting peace and joy you've been searching to find. Whenever you feel down and don't know what to do, just look back to this day and remember all that I have done for you. Let the peace of my love guide you from day to day. Take time to talk with me, in other words, pray! I will never leave you or take my love away. I've invested my time and blood in you to let you slip away. Come to me with all our burdens and cares; look in your heart for me. I will always be there.

Rhontina Burroughs

THE LOCKSMITH

Remembering the day I feel in love with you, my heart was broken, battered and bruised. I was afraid to give and receive love. My heart was closed, but yet you came and searched out my pain, and like a skilled locksmith you unlocked the sealed doors of my existence. You entered me so swiftly and picked up the pieces of my heart and shaped them to your love. Now my essence is open to you. I am able to love, care and hope freely. My pain is no longer locked up, but free-gone.

To you, I thank you, my lover, my friend, my locksmith. This special feeling is a feeling I will cherish forever more

DEAR LOVE

I've been unfaithful to my love. I promised to love only Him, serve Him, obey and trust Him; to put no other before him and dedicate my life to Him. In return, he promised to provide, care, and love me unconditionally. He has committed himself faithfully to me, but I have not done the same for Him. I do not know what happened in my relationship with Him. On the inside, I love Him with all of my heart, mind, spirit and soul. But, the surface side of me reveals something different. I was enticed and deceived by another man. A man that does not love or care about me, provide for me or cherish me. He only wanted what he could take from me, leaving me joyless, unclean, chained and bound.

The man I've been unfaithful to still loves me even though I have hurt him. He continues to shower me with his goodness far beyond my eyes can see.

So why was I unfaithful to him? I have no excuse to give. It's the enemy that enticed me; that made me hurt the one I love. I pray that he forgives me for my fallen state, and takes me back into his heart, to comfort my broken spirit and give me a new start. This time I truly know now what it means to be loved and cared for.

Starting today, I'm going to renew my vows and commitments to Him, because He has renewed His with me.

I love you my Lord and I thank you for loving me

Yours Always,

Rhontina

Rhontina Burroughs

AGAIN

I came to Him just as I was, broken; some parts
of me bruised others weary and worn.

The mask on my face was a permanent fixture. I
hid all of my deep rooted pain and anguish. My
spirit fearful not wanting to trust and love.

I came to Him,

He looked at me, accepted me and began to love me. I
rejected him, closed myself off from Him, and sabotaged
my relationship with Him because of fear.

He presented himself to me, His arms open,
accepting me once again, again and again.

Slowly I began to realize that he loved me despite
all of my fears, hurts, and insecurities. He loved me,
even when I wasn't sure if I wanted His. He gave his
affections to me in spite of objections from me.

He loves me and I have found out what it means to love
Him. The mask on my face has been removed forever,
and replace with smiles of joy and contentment. My
life is free and soaring knowing my God loves me

Unconditionally

R. Burroughs

JOURNEY 2

AT ODDS PT 2

After several years of being apart, I and me decided to converse. There was awkwardness about us. Both of us were guarded, shielding ourselves from the hurt and shame we caused each other. I had changed physically, lost weight and altered my body to be accepted by the masses. Me didn't recognize the new woman that now stood in front of her. She felt abandoned, rejected, brokenhearted, and wounded from our separation. I embraced the new woman I was becoming. I no longer felt padded and weighed down, but somehow free. I was still hurting from the breakup of me, but didn't want anyone to know because they wouldn't understand or so I thought. I was changing, and I desperately wanted me back. I didn't know how to ask and receive her back inside. I tried to welcome her back, but she sadly shook her head no, and said not now- you're not ready to accept me, because I have changed also. I see things much differently from the way I used to. She looked at me compassionately and said you hurt me! I looked at her in the mirror with tears in my eyes and said "I know", will you please forgive me?

R. Burroughs

SPIRITUAL MATH

GW + YL-J+P(3)xF=DM

God's Will + Your Life - Junk + Prayer, Petition and Praise x Faith=Desires Met

God's will **(GW)** for our lives is that we are saved by the blood of Jesus Christ.

+

Your Life **(YL)** You must align your life to God's will. God's word says He knows the plans he has for us. But we must seek him in order to align our will to his.

−

All the JUNK **(J)** in our lives (anger, fear, doubt, bitterness, insecurity, selfishness etc.) Anything that hinders your relationship with God and his plans for you should be place on the altar.

+

Prayer X Petition X Praise

Always pray to God, about anything and everything, every situation. Petition God make your request known to him. Then praise him for what he has done for you, how he has opened doors for you, protected you and guided you. Praise him for his goodness, mercy and favor over your life.

Your **Faith** (**F**) Have faith that God has answered your prayers, step out of your comfort zones, and hold fast to the dream that God has given you. His word tells us to have mustard seed faith.

=

Desires Met

God will give you the desires of your heart, in his time. Don't give up on God. He has your best interest at heart. He will give you that secret longing of your heart when he is ready to give it to you.

Have Faith and Trust God and Receive his blessings for you!!!

DISCOVERED PASSION

Discover by definition means to find. Passion by definition means to have a strong feeling or excitement towards someone or something.

My interpretation of discover means to uncover, or expose; and passion means a desire that reaches beyond the physical encompassing your total being and thought..... With my writings, I have uncovered and exposed a passion that lay dormant for so long. It manifested itself in a way that took me totally by surprise. My writings; is a compilation of writings and poetry that have been written over the years. It explores the topics of self-discovery, purpose, spirituality, love relationships and intimacy. It is my desire that you read with an open mind and awareness.

I present to you, A Discovered Passion!!!

MULTIPLE

There are some many women residing in me, with their own unique gifts, talents, joys and pains; ready, willing and wanting so desperately to come forth and experience all that life has to offer and gain.

Woman #1 is a writer and author of poetry

Woman #2 is a motivational speaker

Woman#3 is an artist and painter

Woman #4 is a teacher

Woman #5 is a medical practioner

Woman #6 desires to be a wife and mother

Woman #7 has been acknowledged as a minister of the gospel; because of her aura and the God in her.

Woman #8 is a business owner

Then there's me! How do I open up and set these women free, when there are so many of them and only one of me? How do I satisfy each of these women's' goals and dreams and at the same time develop me. I must confess, I hear them screaming loudly at me to open up and set them free. But, when I look in the mirror and I see me, I bow my head humbly; promising each of them that they will have their say. Just be patient and continue to pray for me, as I gather my courage and begin to embrace the new becoming of me.

Rhontina Burroughs

STEPPING OUT

Stepping out on faith is the hardest thing to do. You know what to do, how to do, try to encourage others to do the same things that you know you need to do for yourself. You see the gifts, talents, and potential in others, but what about you? God has blessed us all with special desires, passions, abilities, capabilities, possibilities and dreams. All we have to do is what he commands us to do and that is to step out and claim what he has for us.

THINKING

When I think of you, a smile comes to my face. A smile comes to my face because of all of the things you have done for me that I didn't deserve. I smile because you have given me something that I didn't have to,

Beg for

Borrow from

Steal to get

Compromise to have in exchange for something else

You have given me something that is very valuable and cherishable. You have given me love; unconditional, and unshakeable.

You loved me when I didn't deserve to be

You loved me and cared for me when I dint love myself.

You loved me when I gave my heart, love and affections to another.

I smile because you cared so much for me that you searched me out of the multitude, pulled me from the clutches of despair and claimed me giving me new joy.

What have I done that was so great to receive what you have given to me- nothing!

I smile again because of how I feel for you. I know that I can't repay you for what you have done for me- but what I can do is smile when I

Honor You

Praise you and

Worship You

Rhontina Burroughs

ORIGINAL ORIGIN

In the beginning, God said let us make man in our image, and then he looked at man and said it is not good for man to be alone. So he made me; Woman! The complete opposite of man filled with purpose and a plan.

Not to compete against him, but to assist and complete him.

Woman! me! made from God's love! sent from heaven above. Woman! a chosen member of Gods royal society. A body of unique individuals fearfully and wonderfully made, blessed by the Almighty- designed, fashioned, equipped, sculpted, powerful, confident and strong. Never weak! All life and generations flow from and through me.

Woman! That's me!!, there is no one before me, all others come after me.

I Am Genesis! I am Genesis! I Am Gods Princess!

I am an introduction, a promise fulfilled, presented for the first time, all of heaven smiled with zeal! I am not a carbon copy, but an original presentation of God's divine mind.

My body, every mole, curve, bump, lump and freckle, is just the way the creator designed me to be; a blessing for all to see.

God is my source, my strength, my designer, my lifeline; He is my foundation, my root and my core

A multitude of blessings he has in store.

I am His child, the center of His joy!

I am Woman- designed, whole and complete

I am Woman an important part of Gods plan, I am Woman taken from a piece of man.

I am his soulmate, his helpmeet, his woman!

I am Woman. conceived from the mind of How Great Thou ART!

and I am a woman after God's own heart!

JOURNEY 3

FEAR

Fear is a tiny four letter word, but, yet it has so much power. Fear causes immobility, anxiety, and confusion. Fear is associated with dread, fright alarm and panic. This tiny word, yet we give it so much power over us! We are afraid of so many things, for example, flying, bugs worms, all kinds of bugs, public speaking, you name it, there is a fear attached to it. Why do we fear? The bible tells us in 2Timothy1:7, that God did not give us a spirit of fear. God gave us a sound mind. He said "let this mind be in you that is also in Christ Jesus. Jesus didn't have fear so why do we? He encourages us through his word not to be afraid. Isaiah 41:10 says: So do not fear, for I am with you; do not be dismayed, for I am your God. I will strengthen you and help you; I will uphold you with my righteous right hand. So again, why do we fear? We fear because the enemy can't stand for us to have power. His main job is to kill, steal destroy and abort. If we recognize the power that God has given us that will diminish the control that satan has over us.

Secondly, we operate in fear because we do not want to be held accountable. It is so easy to say I'm scared of something, rather than try to overcome it, because people will not question you, if they do, then they will have to face their own fears.

Lastly, we fear as a result of our own insecurities. We know our capabilities, abilities and possibilities; however, we feel that many people can do a much better job at what we are called to do than we ourselves.

So how do we become women of God without fear?

To become a woman of God without fear youneed to step out-

Step out of your comfort zones; step out of yourselves and take off the layers of limitations, restrictions and insecurities off and lay them at the altar.

Embrace a new way of thinking, relating, and reacting to situations, in other words Change!

To become a woman of God without fear; seek out other women to mentor you, encourage you, and inspire you.

To become a woman of God you must be your own cheerleader!!

Tomorrow morning, as you embrace the day, and say your prayers, look yourself in the mirror and say to yourself. I am the daughter of the most high God!! Then point to yourself in the mirror and say loudly!

You Go Girl!!

PREGNANT WITH A CAUSE

The average pregnancy from conception to childbirth, takes 266 days, 36-38 weeks, or 3 trimesters all totaling nine months. Each of us has a dream or desire, that has been conceived in our minds, that demands to birthed, brought forth, called upon, and must come only through us. God has placed many dreams and visions in us to help meet the needs of others. How long have you been pregnant? How long will it take for you to birth your baby? Your "baby" is your dream, or desire, your secret project; your spirit whispers the name of it to you, you see visions of it. It has been on your mind and in your heart. Your baby has been in the womb of seclusion for too long. It is time to go into labor. Labor can be a painful, and scary experience, but you must go through in order to birth your project. It's time to push out your dream, desire or goal. You have to push through obstacles, push through trials, frustrations and fears. The bible says in John 16:21-23(NIV) A woman giving birth to a child has pain because her time has come; but when her baby is born she forgets the anguish because of her joy that a child is born into the world. A woman stands at the door of death to bring a child into the world. What door(s) of adversity must you go through? When you are about to give birth to your dream, adversity in every form will come against you to prevent you from giving birth. That is the subtle plan of the enemy, to prevent, to destroy, to nullify. I must admit as I write this, I too have been pregnant for quite some time with projects, that I have been afraid to birth for fear that I was not equipped to handle the prospect of "motherhood". I would not allow myself to trust others, or my skill level to venture out and explore options that were readily available to me. I realize now that in order to birth my babies, I must step out of the darkness and grab hold of God's hand and fully trust and surrender everything to him. I am finally ready to go through the birthing process; I've had several miscarriages in my life (doubts, lack of confidence, etc) that prevented me from embracing what God has for me. I am ready to share and give my babies to others in the various ways that God sees useful. My children are ready to come forth! What about yours?

THE CHOICE

How many times have you rehearsed, reminisced or found yourself in a reverie about the past? How many times have you said "Oh, if I could only go back to my early years, I would do things differently, change some things, or I would make better choices, decisions or discoveries? I would do more or less, experience more, the list goes on. Throughout our lives, we have made so many excuses as to why we never did, said, or embarked on the activities we so wanted to do. I can imagine God saying to himself, "Oh my child, why do have so little faith in yourself, When I am your propeller and promoter" We fill the church pews every Tuesday, Wednesday, Saturday, and especially on Sunday for some type of study to enrich our lives, we become our own cheerleaders and cheerleaders for others by encouraging them to have faith and receive God's blessings, but once we step outside of the church walls, into the real world, we become afraid and paralyzed. We become victims, we are addicted to being victims, and we begin to lack courage and confidence in ourselves and our God. But we have victory over everything in our lives and we don't have to accept the victim mentality any longer. The encouraging word is found in 1st Corinthians 15:57- But thanks be to God! He gives us the victory through our Lord Jesus Christ. God states in Romans 8:37, that we are more than conquerors through him that loved us. We are victorious! God also states that if we have the faith of a mustard seed, ask for what we desire, we can have what we ask for. But in asking, we must do the work. We must put ourselves in alignment with God's word. We must speak over ourselves. We must encourage ourselves and others. We must believe the promises that God has given us. Romans 8:31 says that if God be for us, then who can be against us? We must stand on that word. That if God is for us (you) then no one, No one can be against us. God is our strength, voice, fighter, everything, God is everything that you need him to be.

I urge you to stop the shoulda, coulda, woulda, train of regret and accept/choose this day to let go of the fears, doubts and limitations of yesterday and yesteryear. Choose this day to make better, wiser, and clearer choices and decisions for your life, take on a more active role in activating your dreams instead of sitting on the sidelines waiting. Joshua 24:15 says choose this day! Who are you going to serve? The old way or the new way. The choice is yours- But as for me and my household, We (I) will serve the Lord and embrace the new.

SEASON, SEASONING, SEASONED

We all love to cook, to show off our best dishes for our loved ones and friends to sample. Some may be a novice in the realm of cooking, while others may be an expert. Cooking or preparing a meal takes preparation, time and dedication. Your flavors have to be just right in order to satisfy ones palate. I want to ask "What's in your seasoning packet?" Seasoning is the usage of various spices and herbs to intensify food flavor. Salt is used universally as a seasoning. Salt is an additive, it is used in conjunction with other flavors to preserve, enhance, magnify, and compliment. The bible says in Matthew 5:13-16, that we are the salt of the earth; but if salt has lost its taste, how can it be made salty again? It is no longer good for anything. God says we are the salt of the earth; we are to keep each other in the faith. God wants us to enhance the body of Christ by leading others to Him. He wants to magnify Him constantly individually and collectively as a spiritual body, and lastly He wants us to compliment (encourage, appreciate, support, respect) each other as Christians by being of good cheer, always pleasant to be around. 1Thessalonians 5:11 says to encourage your brother/sister; Philippians 1:3-6 says to always pray with joy. The bible also emphasizes in Proverbs 27:2 Let another praise you, and not your own mouth; A stranger and not your own lips. So again, what's in your seasoning packet? What spices are you using in your life to preserve, enhance, magnify and compliment others, but mostly God? Here are some questions to think about the next you are preparing your meal for others. (1) Does your seasoning packet consist of too many "hot" spices? Such as harshness in your tone of speech; attitude, insensitivity, sarcasm, bitterness? If so, check your packet! (2) Does your seasoning packet consist of not enough of something? Such as doubt, insecurity, lack of faith, if so, check your packet! (3) Does your seasoning consist of too much self? Low self-esteem, self-absorption, and egotism, if so check your packet! Lastly, (4) Does your packet consist of Galatians 5:22-23,But the fruit of the Spirit is love, joy, peace, forbearance, kindness, goodness, faithfulness, gentleness and self-control. If so, you have the right seasoning blend! Remember you are Gods chosen people. His salt; so, be effective in all that you do, say, think, and relate to others. God is depending on you to serve the perfect meal.

Rhontina Burroughs
May 24, 2014

THE GARDEN

Gardening is a year round project for most people. There are some people who are blessed with a green thumb, while others are not. Those who are gardeners can make anything grow and be able to sustain it. Avid gardeners know the perfect time to plant and harvest their crops. The bible teaches that there is a time for everything. There are certain fruits, vegetables, and flowers that can only be grown during certain seasons of the year. Gardening is a twofold process: Physical and spiritual. The physical side of gardening entails soil, seeds, water, temperature, timing, and hard work. The spiritual side teaches us about faith, hope, help, and patience.

Gardening teaches us about faith by taking the seed as small as they are and planting them in the ground. You hope they grow, you help them to grow, but, most of all, you have to be patient with the growth process.

You are the gardener in your garden. God has given you the seeds (time, talents, and abilities) to plant in your garden of life. He has given you everything you need to grow your garden and to be a good steward over what He has given you. 1 Corinthians 3:8-9(NIV) says, the one who plants and the one who waters have one purpose, and they will each be rewarded according to their labor. For we are co-workers in God's service; you are God's field, God's building.

What are you doing to cultivate your garden? Do you have the proper tools for your garden? Your tools are reading God's word daily, meditating, developing study time, praying and attending bible study.

Secondly, do you till your garden of weeds that stifle or stunt your spiritual growth? Your weeds are: anger, bitterness, jealousy, unforgiveness, doubt and a host of others.

Rhontina Burroughs

Thirdly, do you keep pests out of your garden? You know unauthorized people who give ungodly advice or feed your spirit with negativity.

If you are not doing daily maintenance on your spiritual garden, how do you expect to have a showcase of beauty exemplifying the fruits of the Holy Spirit? Galatians 5:22-23(NIV) says, But the fruit of the Spirit is love, joy peace, forbearance, kindness, goodness, faithfulness, gentleness and self-control. Against such there is no law.

Remember, as you grow your garden, ask God to help you to be the best steward over your garden. Ask Him to help you plant your seeds of faith in all that you do, and continually thank Him for His daily showers of blessings.

A DIVINE APPOINTMENT

Some people come into our lives for a specific reason, but little do we realize that it is only for an appointed season. God in his infinite wisdom knows that someone needs to know Him and His son. So he will be sending you to places where He can be glorified, manifested and represented in the fullest capacity, to bring forth his love enthusiastically.

Your unique personality coupled with your dedication and commitment has encouraged us all, as God's grace and mercy prepares you to rise up and stand tall.

You have shown that if you put faith and trust in God above, he will guide, lift, and hold you with his everlasting love.

But the most important job that God has for you is to look after those he will send to you. You will be a friend, an encourager, an intercessor and motivator just to name a few, God has equipped you with the gifts you need to allow others to be blessed by you.

You have done the job God had for you at this point and time, it's time for you to leave and unite with another place to allow your light to shine.

Remember wherever you go, and whatever you do, God will always be there to see you through.

R. Burroughs

AM I MY SISTAHS KEEPER?

Am I my sister's keeper when I talk about
her looks or her body shape?

Am I my sister's keeper when I don't allow her to be
herself and encourage her to be and do her best?

Am I my sister's keeper when I secretly harbor jealousy and
envy towards her in my heart over her fortune or blessing?

Am I my sister's keeper when I lie to her about anything,
or make her feel that she can't trust me?

Am I my sister's keeper when I refuse to show emotion
towards her in her time of need or shed a tear with her,
pray with her and for her when her spirit is broken?

My sister is a reflection of me! She encompasses aloof
the attributes that the creator has placed inside of me.
In other words, I need her, and she needs me.

She, like me, is a gift from God, placed on
this earth to fulfill life's journey.

Whether we are black, white, or from another
land, we were all created by God's hand

The bible encourages us to love one another as if we were
kin, not judge each other based on the color of skin

We go through the same seasons or stages in life, her struggles as a woman, are my struggles as a woman.

We share a common bond, we are women, we are sisters

Am I my sister's keeper!?

Yes, I am

Even if she doesn't look like me!

R. Burroughs

ENCOURAGING ONE ANOTHER

*The Adversary is the source of all discouragement, discontentment, and doubt. We as Christians, must be vigilant in recognizing the subtle attacks that the enemy hurls at us on a daily basis. But thanks be to God that He gives us comfort, joy, and encouragement through his holy word. Not only can we encourage ourselves, when we are down trodden, but we can also strengthen our sisters when they need a word of encouragement. Come with me as we learn how to become vessels of **encouragement** together!!*

RLB

THE GREAT COMMAND

Train up a child in the way he should go and when he gets old he will not depart from it. Train means to teach, shape, mold, to impart knowledge from the teacher to the student. Jesus is the master teacher, we are merely his students. The Bible gives us many teachable moments to sculpt us the way the creator wants us to be. Every experience, opportunity, and circumstance is and can be a teaching lesson for us to follow. God has given his creation the awesome task of teaching and reaching his children. It is up to us as educators, whether as parents or teachers to educate our children, prepare them for life, the ways of the world, and about Christ. Teaching students can be rewarding, challenging, and frustrating at times, but it is the spark, the ignition, the burning desire that we have to continue to help a child\ student reach his full potential. The African proverb says that it takes a village to raise a child. We teachers, are the village, we must educate our children in every way possible; in season and out. Teachers, you set the precedence for all other occupations. It is through the fundamental years of learning that all learning takes place. For the early educators who have paved the way for us, we can thank you. For the teachers that have inspired you and me today, we thank you for your hard work, service, and sacrifice. You have inspired many to enter the field of education and many other occupations because of the teachings you gave to us. Without you motivating us and challenging us to be the best that we can be, we would not be!! Thank you for all you've done.

Rhontina Burroughs

WE ARE HISTORY

Deuteronomy 14: 2 says; for you are a people holy to the Lord your God. Out of all the peoples on the face of the earth, the Lord has chosen you to be his treasured possession.

We are brothers and sisters sharing one common bond, our roots are strong from the distant land of Africa and beyond.

We are descendants of a royal nation; our heritage is rich of strength, pride, elegance, and grace. Our beautiful black skin encompasses many hues and shades; colors of Gods rainbow by His hands we were divinely made.

We were brought here against our own free will, but God had a plan in the making that only we could fulfill.

We've endured the chains, the lashes, the beatings, the ignorant name calling, and the disrespect against our people. We've lived through the struggles, pushed past pain and fears, demanded equality and justice for all, while shedding some tears.

We have excelled in various occupations in this great land, even the most coveted, prestigious office known to man was part of Gods perfect plan.

With the prayers and determination of our forefathers and mothers, and the guidance of God our father we have persevered, we have overcome, we have achieved. We desired change, we moved forward and won!

We are Black!

We are strong!

We are American!

Our Lives matter!

Our Black lives matter!!

We will forever have a vital role in this society, we are, and we made, and will continue to make history!!

THERE'S VICTORY IN ME

There's victory in me

far more than my eyes can see

God has invested so much into me

That I can't allow myself to be chained or
bound by what society dictates to me.

God has given me power and might to
stand against my fears and fight

I must work hard and stand guard over all I need to
protect in order to have dignity and self-respect

With my head held high, I can do all that my God requires
me to do, I will give Him praise in all I go through

I accept the work, passion, and vision He has for me

I will bless others by what He gives me!

I will forever thank Him for revealing

that He has my future in His hands and that

There is Victory for Me!!

FRIENDS

There have been numerous songs sung about them, poems written about them, television shows and movies portraying them from budding childhood friendships, to end of life friendships. Friends are an extension of who we are. We invite them into our lives; to validate us, to celebrate with us, to share our feelings with, and to accept us; but most importantly to love us. Friends are important to us; and we to them. But out of all the friends we have –there is one who encompasses all of the attributes that we look for and seek out in others. His name is Jesus. Jesus says in John 15:14 you are my friends if you do what I command you. What is Jesus' command? John 15:12 says to love each other as I loved you. Jesus loves us dearly and longs to be friends with you and me. When searching for a friend ask yourself these questions to see if Jesus qualifies:

1) Is Jesus loyal? **Proverbs 17:17** says yes! A friend is always loyal.

2) Can I trust Him with my innermost secrets? **1 John 11:9 says yes! If we confess our sins to him, he is faithful and just to forgive us and to cleanse us from every wrong.**

3) Will He answer me when I call Him? **Psalms 50:15 says yes! And call on me in the day of trouble; I will deliver (rescue, save, release, free) you. The Lord is good, a refuge in times of trouble. He cares for those who trust in him,**

4) Will He be there for me when I am going through rough times? Can I depend on him? To offer a word of encouragement, pray for me, etc? **Hebrews 13:5 says yes! I will never leave you nor forsake you. Matthew 28:20 says I am always with you!**

5) Does Jesus really love me? **Romans 8:38-39** Says yes! **For I am convinced that nothing can ever separate us from his love. Death can't, and life can't. The angels won't, and all the powers of hell itself cannot keep God's love away. Our fears for today, our worries about tomorrow, or where we are—high above the sky, or in the deepest ocean— nothing will ever be able to separate us from the love of God demonstrated by our Lord Jesus Christ when he died for us.**(Living Bible)

As you can see, Jesus clearly fits the friend till the end category. He is available to you at all times, accepting you and loving you just the way you are. I encourage you today to allow him to be in your circle of friends. Allow him to sit face to face and talk with you like myspace, answer his friend request like Facebook, and include him in your family and friends plan, like sprint!

Written by Rhontina Burroughs
Friends and family program
Hammond Grove Church
2/23/2014

HEAVEN

Our lives ended here on earth, and our new lives began with Jesus!
We tried to hold on as long as we could, but God called us and we
couldn't resist His sweet melodious voice beckoning us to come back
to Him. When we saw Him with His arms opened wide; we ran to
Him our feelings we could not hide. We were overcome with such
joy and enormous emotion that in one swift motion He carried us
to His kingdom place. We looked up at Him, but we could not see
His face, we just felt His love generating from Him and caressing
our face. We looked around heaven, and what did we see? We saw
love in its entire splendor floating around us. We saw love in the
flowers, love in the tress and love in the air. We are surrounded with
God's love and care. We are here in this wonderful place that our
God has prepared for us. It is so gorgeous here, we wish you could
see. We miss all of you, but please do not weep or shed a tear for us,
for we are truly happy. We wanted to share this message with you
to let you know that we will always be around you. We are hovering
over you and watching over you. God has called us from this place
to be in heaven with him; close to Him is where we need to be.

Safe, secure and eternally free.

Dedicated to

Hattie Davis, Willie F. Davis, Theodore Hankerson, Lillian Harper,

Johnny Davis, Mack Hankerson, Naomi
Hankerson, Willard Valdez Pierre Rouse,

Louvenia Rouse

Rhontina Burroughs

DEDICATED TO MACK HANKERSON

The strength, the backbone, the pillar of our
family has graduated from life to death.

He has come full circle of the life that he has been
given. On his way, he inspired, motivated, and
taught lessons and blessing everyone he met.

With his infectious laugh and deep raspy voice, we his family sat
mesmerized listening to his tall tales and jokes, his entrance into
every family get together was greeted by his wet kisses-oh, how we
will miss those kisses and stories. He was always a joy to be around.

What will we do without our pillar?, our strength?

The family bond that we held so close

We family, will carry on!

We will carry on!

Rest in peace, Uncle Mac

We love you

LONGEVITY

-Family Reunion-

Your journey, your circle of life is now complete. You have come full circle of the life that God has planned for you. You have journeyed, paved the way and laid the foundation that we your family must travel today.

As we embark on our journey, we take your spirits with us to lead and guide us. We take your lessons, life skills and love with us as we remember you. We take with us the faith you have left us with to ensure the legacy and longevity of our family. We are forever indebted to you for all you have instilled in us. We honor you, we cherish you, we will always love you and keep you in our hearts.

Written by Rhontina Burroughs

ROOTED AND GROUNDED IN LOVE

There is nothing like family. There is nothing like family. We get together, we have good times, laughs, and remembrances. When we get together we may fuss, argue, or disagree, but at the close of each day, we are family! We have gone through trials, heartaches, triumphs and joys, we have hung in there with each other, fought for each other, and encouraged each other, but most importantly we have love for one another. We are family! We are each other's existence; we are each other's keeper. For if we are without each other, we will not be. We are one united; we are the life of each other. We are the joy of each other. We are all that we have. We are family!!

LIVING THE GOLDEN LIFE

I was young, now I am old and I've never seen the righteous forsaken, nor his seed begging bread. Those powerful yet reflective words were written in the book of psalms expressing the goodness of God. Seniors, did you know that old age is a blessing from God? Proverbs 16:31 says that gray hair is a glorious crown, it is found in the way of the righteous. You seniors have reached the season in your life that symbolizes growth, wisdom, and favor.

Growth is a season, it is an aspect of change. it is a period of development and maturity. Throughout your life, you have grown physically, mentally, educationally, financially, and spiritually. Growing older is a time of reflection, rejoicing and renewal. With growth, comes wisdom.

Wisdom, is the sum of all learning, having good judgement, and understanding. Proverbs 9:10 says the fear of the Lord is the beginning of wisdom, the Lord says that through me, your days will be many. If you are wise, your wisdom will reward you. Your advanced years is/was designed by God to teach the younger generations and to prepare them/us about the world. Lastly, with growth and wisdom comes favour.

Favor is God's blessings over your life, or reward. God's favor over your life has prolonged your progression in life. The Lord says in Isaiah 46:3b, that I have carried you since birth, I've taken care of you since the time you were born. because of God's hand on your life, the bible says in Proverbs 3 that you will find favor with both God and people, and you will earn a good reputation.

So, today, we the younger generation, pay tribute to the contributions, sacrifices, and service that you have given throughout your lives. You have found favor among us, but most importantly you have found favor with God. May God continually shine his face upon you. Amen

Rhontina Burroughs

THE CALLING

Go ye therefore into the nations and minister to others. These words were spoken by the master physician to his disciples; 2000 years later that command still resonates today. The book of John 13:34-35 says: "A new commandment I give to you, that you love one another, even as I have loved you, that you also love one another. By this, all men will know that you are my disciples, if you have love for one another." This is your calling; you were designed, formed and shaped to be a caregiver a life sustainer. You were given this opportunity to make a difference, and to be of service to others and to your creator.

Nurses, did you know that you are God's representatives? You have been given the great command to go out into the community and the world to give the sick and the afflicted a caress of the masters hand.

We see you everywhere, providing care in the hospitals, doctor's offices, schools, clinics, churches and the military. You are the unsung heroes on the front lines of the battle of sickness ministering aid, comfort and dignity to those who were placed in your care. Your desire, commitment, dedication and sacrifice has touched families and given reassurance to those who had lost their will to live.

So, today, Nurses of the Lamar School of Nursing; we honor you, we pay tribute to you because you went out into the world, and participated in the ongoing battle of sickness. You healed, comforted, shed tears and rejoiced with others in their healing. But most importantly, you have set the standard of excellence for nurses that have come and will continue to come after you. You adhered to the scripture which states therefore, my dear brothers and sisters stand firm. Let nothing move you. Always give yourselves fully to the work of the Lord, because you know that your labor in the Lord is not in vain. You have endured, you persevered, you kept the faith and you blessed others by being a nurse.

Written by
Rhontina Burroughs
October 3, 2015
Lamar School of Nursing 20th Reunion

Rhontina Burroughs

PREPARED

Spreading my wings in preparation to fly. I'm like an eagle soaring high. my best life is in front of me, my childhood in the past. I can't wait to embark on this task. So many questions; Will I fit in? Will I do a good job? Have I learned enough to prepare me for this? My answer is YES!!! to all the questions of doubt. Because My father in heaven says I am fear fully and wonderfully made, he didn't give me a spirit of fear, and he didn't bring me this far to leave me. For his word says to me Greater is He that is within me, than he that is without him. So off I go into this new undiscovered land of mine. only God knows what treasures I will find. My faith, my hope, my trust, and my life is in his hands. Thank you my Lord for saving me and preparing me for this journey!!

Be blessed in all that you! may God's face forever shine upon you!

VICTORY

V: Vison- Have a vision for yourself/family/goals

I: Invested/Identity- God has invested His time in you. Know whose child you are.

You are a child of the most High God.

C: Covered-You are covered by the blood of Jesus Christ

T: You are talented; God has blessed you with many hidden talents.

O: Your steps are **ordered** by God

R: Be **Ready** to be used by God

Y: There is no one like **you**!! **You** are an original. God made **you** for a purpose!!

Rhontina Burroughs

JOURNEY 4

DESIRED

My relationship with you has been a wonderful experience. I love how I feel when I'm with you, sexy, alive, and vibrant is how I feel. you hear me, respond to me when I speak to you. You make me feel as if I'm the only woman on the planet honey bless you!!! My womanly charms bring out the hunter in you. My sensuousness makes you want to chase me, and I love it because it makes me step out of me and experience another side of me. My inhibitions are erased when I'm in your presence. Sometimes I feel the women in me are in competition with each other to step up their game to see which one has the greater power. It's all good because they are a part of me. The seductress in me desires to entice, tease, tempt, and motive. The educator in me wants to teach you more of me. The poet in me wants so desperately to write about my experiences with you, in fact I am. This is how I feel when I'm with you. Thank you for bringing out every woman in me!!

COFFEE

To all those who know me, I love me some coffee. I can drink it all day long. Well, I wrote a little something about the love of my life. I dedicate this to you, my sweet!

Coffee is my man in a can! I can have him in the morning, noon day, as an afternoon delight or a midnight night cap.

Coffee is my man in can! I can have him expresso dark or cappuccino crème. Having him in my cup is my dream.

Coffee is my man in a can! I can have him as strong as I need him to be or weak (NOT)!! Don't want any weak coffee. It's just brown water to me! That just won't suit me. His flavorful strong aroma is excitement to me. His scent welcomes and draws me into a hypnotic daze. I need him to bold, pleasurable and flavorful all at the same time to calm the beast in me from time to time.

Coffee is my man in can! I can have him in all flavors from across the land! African, Mexican, Irish Cream, Puerto Rican; just to name a few, it does not matter to me as long as my palate loves the smoothness of the brew.

Coffee is my man in a can! He is my tranquil elixir; one sip of him is my attitude and all day fixer! I can't go too long without him, I will go into withdrawal. He keeps me calm and on point all day long.

What you say!? What you say!? me addicted!? I need a twelve step program! An intervention!? No, I don't! Nope, don't think I do, just need a couple of cups a day to get me through.

Rhontina Burroughs

And, to all of you who don't seem to understand,

I just need my man,

My man in a can!

Let me introduce him to you, His name is

COFFEE!!

THE DILEMMA

Our conversations were very deep, engaging, thought provoking and time consuming. We discussed everything –spirituality, current events, world affairs; even the possibility of….. our flirtations were funny, sneaking glances and soft touches, borderline erotic, with a subtle hint of exotic, leaving us to wonder in our minds, what would happen if we, should we, could we cross the line and explore our passions. We danced around the subject so many times, each time getting closer, closer, closer, until……it happened. We were no longer the same- just like Adam and Eve, we were now naked and ashamed. We had seen each other in a different light, everything we tried to hide, our vulnerabilities, our fears, and doubts were now exposed to each other. What would we do? What did we do? We became afraid and……

DON'T WANNA BEG

Please don't look at me like that, your eyes
penetrates me to the depths of my soul.

Please don't touch me like that, your touch sends
a thousand quivers down my spine.

Please don't whisper my name the way you do, it
makes me want and desire you even more.

Please don't look at me, touch me, or say my name.

Because right now, I'm having a hard time resisting you,

ANGEL

I have always wished for and prayed for God to send me an angel.
Countless days I have looked towards heaven hoping to catch glimpse
of one His celestial beings, my search would always come up empty.

Then one day by divine intervention, you came into my
life and we became the best of friends. God sent you
to me to love me and give me guidance and love.

I thank God for you.

For you see, in all of my searching for an angel, I looked
for the halos, glowing lights streaming from above with
flowing wings; not once did I ever imagine he would
answer by sending someone in physical form.

My eyes have been opened.

My prayers have been answered.

The angel that I prayed for is

You

R. Burroughs

.

CLUELESS

I never knew what love was until I met you

I never knew what a sensual kiss felt like until you kissed me

I never knew a touch could feel so warm, soothing,
and inviting until you touched me

I never knew what it meant to be understood
until you began to understand me

I never knew what it felt like to be held so tenderly until you held me

I never knew how beautiful my name was until you whispered it

I never knew my love was wanted until you asked for it

I never knew that I was the one you needed

Until Now, I've been clueless!!

INVITATION

I've been waiting for you to come and take your rightful place in my life. I have seen glimpses of my life with you. Being with you brings wholeness, oneness, and completion; enough for me to smile with hope. Enough for me to smile with purpose. Enough for me to continually thank God above for you. Come on in, you are invited to finish this unfinished portrait of what life is to be for us.

ANATOMY

You are my favorite subject.

I desire to sit in your classroom and learn about you, study you and dissect you, read about you, explore you, expound on you, explain you, compare/contrast you, test you, quiz you, research more about you, discuss you, write my thesis about you,- for you are one serious topic to discuss. Then put you down and reflect back on what I've studied about you.

Wondering how I can life applicate my life to you!

R. Burroughs

CHILD'S PLAY

You are my-

Z-zest for life

Y-yearning

X-xillieration

W-wonderful wonder

V-validation

U-usher, uniqueness

T-tease and tantalizer

S-strength, sex, soulmate

R-restorer, for you restored love in me

Q-quiet, quality time

P-Provider, protection, promoter, passion

O-openness/oneness

N-navigator for you direct me

M-muse, music, you are the other part of me!

L-lover

K-keeper

J-joy

I-Inspiration

H-helper, honey, hero

G-God given

F-friend

E-Excitement, Eroticism, Enthusiasm, Encourager, Equal

D-desire, delight, my dream

C-cheerleader, coach, comfort, center

B-my beloved

A-all that matters to me!!

You are the ABC's of my life

Rhontina Burroughs

FOR YOU

For all that you have done for me,

I thank you

For the times that I have hurt you and caused you pain

I apologize with all that I am

For all of the times you have stood by me and encouraged me

I am truly grateful

For all that you have given to me, your sacrifices

I am humbled

I am blessed because of you

You did not have to do what you did

I am totally indebted to you

Thank You

I love you

FRESH EYES

Standing before you, smiling, looking at you, happy to see you, ecstatic to be in your company, you look at me as if you've never seen me before. You look at me standing before you half confused, half dazed like a deer caught in headlights. Trying to figure me out; staring at me to see if there is some recognizable feature about me that would familiarize you to me. "I ask is there something wrong"? You respond "no". Taken aback, I ask" How do I look to you"? You respond "like you". I'm dumbfounded. I ask myself. "What does that mean"? I ask myself again, how do or should I respond to that. How EXACTLY does he see me? Pop Quiz- Were you mesmerized by a different side of me? Did you see something in me, on me, or over me that surprised or frightened you? Did my style of dress make you uncomfortable? Was there something about my alter that made you want to question your love, commitment or dedication to me? Your response to me was so unnerving, frightening, and scary for me. Unlike something I've never seen before.

Maybe you're seeing me differently, because I AM different. I am powerful, I am confident

Maybe your vision of me has changed and you're beginning to see the woman I have evolved into.

Maybe, just maybe, you need to check your sight;

And see me again with fresh eyes!

I WONDER

So many times in my life, I've wondered what it would have been like to have never met you.
To have never felt your love for me.
To have never known what it is like to share my thoughts and dreams with you.
To have never felt the caress of your touch.
To have never enjoyed a stimulating conversation with you.
To have never seen your face gleam with happiness and pride.
or............
To have seen the unique person you are inside.
or............
To have never experienced being the one you wanted to share the rest of your life with.
But, as I reminence over our togetherness,
I can't imagine me not sharing my love, my joys, my todays, or tomorrows without you!!
Happy Anniversary
Written by Rhontina Burroughs 6/15/2015

AFRAID

I run because I am afraid to love you.

I hide because I don't want you to see my imperfections and flaws

I cover my eyes because my eyes are the windows to my soul, and I don't want you to see the hurt I hide so deep within

I drown out the sound of your soothing voice because it is like a drug; It calls for me reaching deep

Please don't tell me you love me,

Show me that you do

R. Burroughs

I AM YOUR MAN

Every woman would love to hear these words spoken by the man of her dreams; and every man who truly loves his woman would love to speak these words. Here's a little help: I dedicate this to every woman. Enjoy!

Woman,

I am yours

I am your prince

I am your lover and your friend

I am the one God has sent to you-for you to depend

He has equipped me with everything you need

I am yours, totally-My feelings for you; I will not hide.

Share yourself with me-with me you can confide

Your joys are my joys

Your pains are my pains

With me you will have happiness and all there is to gain

I will be there to love and protect you

I will never reject you; for if I don't uphold and cherish you, then I as a man will fail at what God has designed me to do.

God is my king; I am merely His subject-

I submit myself to Him, so that I may be of unyielding service, commitment and dedication to you. The love that God has given me allows me to shower it on you.

Take what you need from me; allow me to minister to you the way you minister to me

I Am your Man-

Bring me your desires, and let my love touch your heart

I AM YOUR WOMAN

I am your woman,

Sent from God above, inside of me is a treasure chest full of love.

In me you can find rest and peace, comfort for your mind and soul.

Give your heat to me and forever I will uphold.

With me there is no need to hide, take off your mask black man and lay it aside.

Allow me to see the real you that God intended you to be, not what society or your masculinity expects you to be.

I am your well. Draw your strength from me; for the well I draw I draw my strength comes from the one who created me.

He brought me from the core of your being to complete and fulfill you.

I submit myself to Him, therefore I submit myself to you.

I am your woman sent from God above to be a helpmeet to you and bring forth His love.

INSATIABLE ME

May I have some of you? I'm a little greedy so a little won't do. I need an ample dose of you to keep functioning, you understand don't you?

I don't want an appetizer, it will only make me
mad and irritable, it just a tease, a sample,

I don't want a meal before the meal. I tend to get
satisfied to quickly, I want the whole entree

Enough that will last me

I told you I was greedy.

Now back to my original question?

May I have some..... of....... You!!

Rhontina Burroughs

LIFETIME

Once in a lifetime, there comes a love so strong, so satisfying and fulfilling that I agree with God, and take a step back, smile and say "Yes, this is good" It is a joy that unspeakable, a faith in love that is unshakeable, and a life together that is unbreakable and inseparable. I am so happy; happiness has found me, claimed me and accepted me! I am so grateful for all that God has given. I am one with God; I am now one with you. We are now three.

YESTERDAY, TODAY, TOMORROW

Do you remember the first time we met? The first time we held hands? The first time you told me you loved? The first time we stood before God and man and made a vow to each other, to love honor and keep each other as long as we both live? We were so young and carefree, ready to face the world you and me. Over the years, we have shared many first together. Some good, some bad, but through it all, I will forever cherish each one of our first of yesterday.

Today, years later as I stand with you to reaffirm my vows and love for you, I am reminded of what drew us together. Was it your charm, your conversation, your wit? Maybe it was how you related to me and how you made me feel. I don't know, but God knew. He knew I need someone just like you to love, pray for me, and understand me the way you do. It was His divine plan that we were meant to be and continue to be one with each other. I am so happy to have you by my side, you my husband and I your bride. Today, we will start a new chapter in our lives, filled with new hopes, dreams, desires, and passions for one another, you, me, us, our family-adding on to the foundation we started, continuing the ongoing legacy legacy we have created. Like a fine wine we have gotten better with time. We are a treasure chest full of love, devotion, and happiness; a time piece of history, that can't be measured. I can't wait to share my tomorrows with you.

And even though tomorrow is not promised to either one of us, I pray it is Gods will for us to see another year of you and me, until we are old and gray remembering back to our first day of yesterday, embracing each other faithfully.

Rhontina Burroughs

LOVING YOU

I'm in love

I'm in love

As I stand before you; looking at you

I can truly say, that I love you

I now know what love is.

Love is you taking my hand, placing it inside of yours, holding it;
our fingers entwined together letting me know we are linked as one.

Love is you seeing me, all of me and accepting me,
cherishing me and claiming me as your one and only.

Love is us standing before God, angels and this
assembly to declare our love for each other, and to
thank God our father for joining us together.

Love is me, you, us, embarking on our future

Together

ME AND YOU

To you, I am like a hidden treasure, ready to be opened and explored.

To me, you are like an open book of poetry ready to be read and recited like haiku.

To you, I am like a vintage wine ready to be opened and savored at the proper time.

To me, you are like a key that has unlocked the secret door of my core.

To you, I am like the ocean ready to dive in and swim in my rippling love pool.

To me, you are like a musician ready to play a love song.

To you, I am the instrument ready to feel the soft tips of your fingertips, strumming my hair, my body, my intellect, my passions.

To each other we are like the beats of a drum; in tune beating softly to the rhythm of our hearts that only lovers can make.

Rhontina Burroughs

MEETING

Love searched for my heart

Hope knocked on the door of my heart

Faith opened the door to my heart

Peace calmed the anxiety of my heart

Joy surrounded and healed my heart

Happiness met my heart at the alter and joined with another and said

I do!

MERGER

My Company, Burroughs Inc. Is ready to form a new partnership. My company is small, but has growth potential. My company has been in existence 47 years with a solid partnership backed by Trinity services. We offer services that will meet and fulfill your every need. In addition to the benefits received, you will find my companies assets are rewarding and appealing. My company has four very unique employees: I, my, me, and mine respectfully. With a possible merger, we are looking to add three new employees- us, our, and we to our company. This merger will profit both companies to the highest degree with substantial rewards and perks.

The ideal company must be knowledgeable of Trinity services (God, Jesus, and the Holy Spirit) and have a clear understanding of the mission statement of John 3:16 as well as the laws, doctrines and promises of the binding contract.

If you feel that Burroughs Inc. is suitable for your company, please contact Trinity Services at 1.800.yes prayer or email them at Heremyprayer.com or #GodIneedawife for additional information.

MIRROR, MIRROR

You are my reflection,

when I look at me, I see you.

When I speak I hear your voice. When I think about me, and my future, I think of you.

You are my friend, my confidant,

You are my prayers answered

Your are the puzzle piece that fits securely in my life!

MY LIFE TO YOU

When God made Adam, He took a rib from his side, to show
that he would be incomplete without his helpmeet. Since that
fateful day in the garden man has searched endlessly for that
one piece that was missing from him. I too have been in a state
of loneliness, my mind in a daze wandering around aimlessly
as if in a daze, anticipating when my mate would appear to me.
Today, as I stand before you, my search is over. Gods, gift to me,
now stands before me. I can say like Adam- My Woman! You are
flesh of flesh and bone of my bone. God has given you to me to
complete me; that hollow empty place in my body has been filled,
my side no longer aches because God given me my rib. My life, my
space is now peaceful because you are in it. I am proud to stand
before you today a complete man. I am now your husband!

Rhontina Burroughs

NO MORE

Trying my best not call you to hear your voice.

Trying not to miss you.

Your absence leaves me with an incompleteness that engulfs every part of me. There is a lack of connectedness, cohesiveness, balance and structure.

My aura is depleted like the gloom of the sky without the rays of the sun.

You are that other piece of me. My equal.

Without you in my life,

I'm empty

REALIZATION

Went to David's Bridal yesterday, sat in the car, pondered getting out and going in. I saw women young and old, smiling, laughing, and joyful as they entered in the building; ready to look at, try on, and fantasize about the glorious day when all eyes are on them and the One that chose them.

I went to David's Bridal sat in my car, afraid to go in because what if I saw someone that I knew, how would I explain that…….

I went to David's Bridal sat in my car and shed a tear, because I felt cheated out of something that I always wanted. I yearned for it to be me that was looking at the beautiful dresses, trying on dresses, feeling the fabric against my warm skin.

I went to David's Bridal sat in my car and became mad as hell with myself because I allowed myself to be cheated out of what I truly wanted, desired, and yearned for by staying in an unproductive relationship for far too long.

I went to David's Bridal sat in my car, pondered going in, then I looked up towards heaven and said "Lord I'm not ready yet, prepare **me** to receive what you have for me".

SHAME YOU LOST ME

The one my heart belongs to continues to seek love outside of me. He can draw what he needs from my well, which is pure and unadulterterated, but I can't draw the same from his. His well is stagnant and murky. There is no life sustainability. In the prime of our union, I drew from him, fertilized my seeds from him; but alas, was unable to procreate more. I saw where we were when his love walked out the door. He tries to come back every now and again, guilt does a wonderful thing to the heart and mind by making one realize the treasure he once had. But as for me, I am doing just fine

THE DIFFERENCE

I need, want, and desire to be married. I want to be married because of my weariness of being alone. I want to be married, because I feel that I'm mature enough, woman enough, and know enough about marriage to be able sustain and maintain my relationship intact. In fact, I have observed enough marriages and listened to their woes not to make the same mistakes. I tell you. I want to be married. I've read enough books and attended more than my share of woman's conferences and sat in on a few marriage sessions to write my own books about relationships. I'll say it again, I want to be married. I want to be married because it is hard being single in a couple's world. Its difficult cooking for one, only you get to enjoy it. It's not the best arrangement at times being alone in your house when you want to feel protected. Don't get me wrong, I know how to survive, make a living, pay my bills, and take care of myself; I want someone to take care of me too. I get oh so tired of sleeping in my queen size bed, Alone! I'm ready to upgrade to a king sized bed with my King in it! In other words, I want a king in my palace to help me rule over my Queendom. I can go on and on about my wants, let's be clear I want to be married. I know the difference between wants and needs. Want is something that is wished for; something that you can live without. Want is something that is in addition to. Which brings me to need. Need is something that is required. Let me explain, I need to pay off my bills (required), but I want a new flat screen TV. Or, I need to drink more water (required) but I want a cup of coffee with an expresso shot. I clearly know the difference. I need to be married because it is essential to my livelihood. It is essential because I was designed to be yoked to my mate. To be his helpmeet, his lover, his queen, his confidant, his everything. I need to be married because I am old fashioned. I believe in the sanctity of marriage. I believe that it is Gods will for male and female to work together as one body to fulfill a purpose, to love each unconditionally and be responsible for each other, removing selfishness in us. God created marriage for his glory and for our good. The bible says it is not good for man (woman) to be alone. I truly believe that, because he made us (me) to relational not only to him but to others. Finally, I desire to be married, simply because it has always been my desire to married and raise a family with my husband. The bible says in Proverbs, Delight yourselves in the Lord, and He shall give you the desires of your heart. God knows my heart and He knows my desire. I'm trusting him and His word. Desire is a strong word because it means to long for; to crave, I won't say that I crave marriage, but I do long for the intense companionship, and the ability to minister to my husband and him to me. Simply put; I desire to be married because I want and need to be for the reasons stated, I am ready, willing and able to give myself totally, to love, care for, cherish and motivate the man God sends to me. Even though I am whole and complete with God. The mate he sends to me will be an added bonus to what God has already given to me.

THE MAN, HIS LADY, THEIR COUNTRY

The bible says in Ephesians 5:22-23 that a husband should love his wife as Christ has loved the church; and gave himself for it. The Unites States military and marriage are based on the fundamentals of God's word and law. Our union of love is joined together by the combining of the United States flag and our ceremonial bands. On this day, we pledge to uphold the promises of our God as well as the military's standards. We look to our rings and the flag to symbolize our belief in life and the eternal, to always remember those who have paved the way for us. Keeping in mind united we will stand as a family, and divided we will fall.

We pledge today the words of Ruth 1:16(NIV) for wherever you go, I will go and wherever you lodge, I will lodge; your people shall be my people, and your God, my God. On this day, our household will be one nation under God; as we join together with the bonds of the United States flag and circular rings, We pray to God our Father to keep us safe, to exemplify Christ every day in our marriage and to minister to others at home and abroad. We will forever remember this union day, and reflect on our nation's motto and our personal creed.

In God We Trust

Amen

TOGETHER

We began our romantic career with other at the height of our
budding years. We were just beginning to explore the fundamentals
of our relationship. We were each first, from the innocence of
flirtation to the experimental consummation. We have grown
together, experienced outside only to come back to the confines of
what we shared and started so long ago, not wanting to let each
other go. We are a tradition, a relic, and a treasure; with a love so
strong it can't be measured. We are comfortable with each other, we
know each other. No matter come what may, we will always know
how to return back to our rightful place... in each other's lives

UNFINISHED

He watched and studied her intently as she slept. He admired her body frame. He inhaled her scent. He noticed every flaw, imperfection and detail of her. He took a mental snapshot of her total being. He memorized every moan, groan, sigh, and whimper. Every sound that escaped from her lips made him stand to attention. He wondered to himself, what was it about her that evoked such passion in him that made him want to protect, nurture, provide and care for? What was it about this magnificent creature that made him smile and delight in her beauty? He thought to himself the words penned in Zephaniah 3:17; the lord your God is with you, he is mighty to save. He will take great delight in you, he will quiet you with his love, he will rejoice over you with singing. Yes, he delighted and rejoiced over her. He loved her. He desired her. This woman, this mortal, was his creation. He looked upon her and said "That's good".

Rhontina Burroughs

WHO AM I?

Popeye's love was Olive Oil

Superman's secret was Lois Lane

Jacob's Admiration was Rachel

Samson's Weakness was Delilah

David's Desire was Bathsheba

Adam's Rib was Eve

What am I to you?

WONDERING

As, I sit alone looking out my window, my mind begins to wonder, will I find a love to call my own; and if so, how will my lonely heart know? Will I be able to know by the way he looks deep into my eyes and finds the window to my soul; or will I tell by the way he touches my skin and feel the yearning from within? How will this person find me? Will he spot me out of the multitude and beckon my heart to his for a long lasting interlude.....

Will he search high and low, cross the skies and walk the valley low?

How will he find me?

What will I say when he comes?

Welcome to my heart, my love, I knew you would come

Rhontina Burroughs

YEARNING

I need you

I need to be with you

I need to be intimate with you

I need to feel your touch, hear your voice

I need to hear your words of love saturate and penetrate my
heart and flow, flow like a river into the fibers of me.

I need you to hold me, shield me, and be my fortress.

I need you to take my love and combine it with
your and make a covenant for us to enjoy

I need you to need me

I love you

YOUR GIRL

Don't wanna be your go to girl every time sumthin is wrong with you and your girl. You know you and your girl are incompatible, yet you stay with her to satisfy the insatiable appetite that you're being seems to crave.

Don't wanna be that girl that strokes your ego, when she don't make you feel manly,

She is not you're your equal let alone the one that has been set aside just for you-

You know that you have been too blind to see, that I am the one –not she; that's why you keep running back to me. It is I that is your compatible, I am the one you find insatiable.

I am the one you linger around, cause in me everything is found.

But, I don't wanna continue to be the go to girl while you're in a fleeting moment. Don't wanna be that girl that you just have fun with, be cool with and chill with while you're on hiatus from her. I don't want to be that girl that you just run to when you're feeling lost. I wanna be the one that you want to be with at all cost.

I wanna be your one and only.

SAYONARA

I love you but what we have is not enough for you to consider me. What we shared was genuine and I will forever love you, but this **bondage** that I have with you can't go on. When you call I will not answer. I will no longer try to communicate with you. It seems as though I think about you more than you think about me. I think about your feelings more than you think about mine. Life is too short, to be with someone that doesn't make you a priority their life.